Push and Pull

by Emily C. Dawson

amicus readers

1

Amicus Readers are published by Amicus
P.O. Box 1329, Mankato, Minnesota 56002

Printed in the United States of America at Corporate Graphics, North Mankato, Minnesota.

Library of Congress Cataloging-in-Publication Data
Dawson, Emily C.
  Push and pull / by Emily C. Dawson.
      p. cm. -- (Amicus readers. Everyday science)
  Summary: "Describes the forces of push and pull using everyday objects such as strollers
and wagons. Includes experiments"-- Provided by publisher.
  Includes index.
  ISBN 978-1-60753-021-3 (lib. bdg.)
  1. Force and energy--Juvenile literature. I. Title.
  QC73.4.D39 2011
  531'.6--dc22

                                    2010011284

Series Editor   Rebecca Glaser
Series Designer   Mary Herrmann
Photo Researcher   Heather Dreisbach

Photo Credits
Adie Bush/Getty, cover; Caro/Alamy, 14, 15; Claudia Dewald/iStock, 8, 9,
21 (t); Corbis, 5, 21 (b); Digital Vision, 10, 11, 20 (b); Greenland/
Dreamstime.com, 6; Jacob Melrose/Dreamstime.com, 16, 20 (t);
John Kelly/Getty Images, 7; Jupiterimages/Getty Images, 17; Rodger
Tamblyn/Alamy, 12, 13; Stewart Cohen/Getty Images, 1, 19

1222
42010

10 9 8 7 6 5 4 3 2 1

Table of Contents

You cannot see forces. But you can see what happens when forces are at work.

Kevin uses force to push Ethan in the go-cart.

Some forces are push forces.

Sam uses his legs to push the bike pedals.

push

Some forces are
pull forces.

Ava pulls herself across
the monkey bars.

pull

Cassie pushes
the merry-go-round
to make it spin.

The faster she pushes,
the faster it spins.

push

Jacob walks his dog Max.

Max pulls on his leash to sniff a tree.

Jacob pulls Max back.

pull

13

Anna walks to her aunt's house.

She pushes her baby sister in a stroller.

push

Josie and her mom go to the farmer's market.

Josie pulls the fruits and vegetables in her wagon.

farmer's market

Layla pushes her legs and then pulls the swing to go back and forth.

Pushing and pulling forces move the swing.

19

Picture Glossary

farmer's market—an outdoor area where farmers sell fruits, vegetables, flowers, and other things they grow

force—any action that changes how an object is moving

pull—to move something forward or toward you

push—to press something away from you

Ideas for Parents and Teachers

Science and technology aren't just for engineers—we use them every day. *Everyday Science*, an Amicus Readers Level 1 series, introduces children to scientific concepts through familiar situations and objects. The picture glossary and photo labels reinforce new vocabulary. Use the following strategies to help your children predict, read, and comprehend.

Before Reading
- Ask children what things they push and pull.
- Discuss the cover photo and the photo on the title page. What do these photos tell them?
- Look at the picture glossary together. Read and discuss the words.

Read the Book
- Read the book to the children, or have them read independently.
- Show them how to look at the photographs and use the picture glossary to understand the full meaning.

After Reading
- Have the children retell which items are pushed or pulled.
- Try the simple experiments on page 23.
- Prompt the children to think more, asking questions such as *What pushes or pulls big machines like cars or trains? What types of vehicles pull instead of push?*

Experimenting with Push and Pull

Try This:

1. Push a toy car across a hard floor. Now tie a string to the car and pull it. Which was easier, pushing or pulling?

2. Try the same thing again, but with a large toy truck. Did you need more force or less force to make the truck move?

3. Try pushing and pulling the car and truck on carpet or a rug. Was it easier or harder than on the hard floor?

What happened?

1. Both are about the same.

2. The larger the toy, the more force it takes to move.

3. The toys need more force to move on the carpet. The toys and carpet rub against each other. This creates a force called friction that slows things down.

23

Index

Web Sites

BBC School Science Clips—Pushes and Pulls
http://www.bbc.co.uk/schools/scienceclips/ages/
5_6/pushes_pulls.shtml

Motorsport Mathematics: Pushing and Pulling Forces
http://www.racemath.info/forcesandpressure/
ks1_force.htm

Rader's Physics 4 Kids
http://www.physics4kids.com/